ANIMALS
That Make a Difference!

Turtles

Ashley Lee

Explore other books at:
WWW.ENGAGEBOOKS.COM

VANCOUVER, B.C.

↱ WWW.ENGAGEBOOKS.COM

Turtles: Pre-1
Animals That Make a Difference!
Lee, Ashley, 1995
Text © 2025 Engage Books
Design © 2025 Engage Books

Edited by: A.R. Roumanis, and Ashley Lee
Design by: Mandy Christiansen

Text set in Arial Regular.

FIRST EDITION / FIRST PRINTING

library and archives canada cataloguing in publication

Title: Turtles / Ashley Lee.
Names: Lee, Ashley, author.
Description: Series statement: Animals that make a difference

Identifiers: Canadiana (print) 20230448542 | Canadiana (ebook) 20230448569
ISBN 978-1-77878-694-5 (hardcover)
ISBN 978-1-77878-703-4 (softcover)

Subjects:
LCSH: Turtles—Juvenile literature.
LCSH: Human-animal relationships—Juvenile literature.

Classification: LCC QL737.P94 C38 2025 | DDC J599.885—DC23

This project has been made possible in part by the Government of Canada.

Canada

Turtles love
sitting in the sun!

Turtles are covered in a hard shell.

Their shells cannot be taken off.

Some turtles can hide their head and legs in their shells.

Some turtles
have thick feet.

Others have flippers that help them swim.

Some turtles live on land.

Other turtles
live in the water.

Some turtles live on land and in water.

They are found
all over the world.

13

Some turtles eat plants and some eat animals.

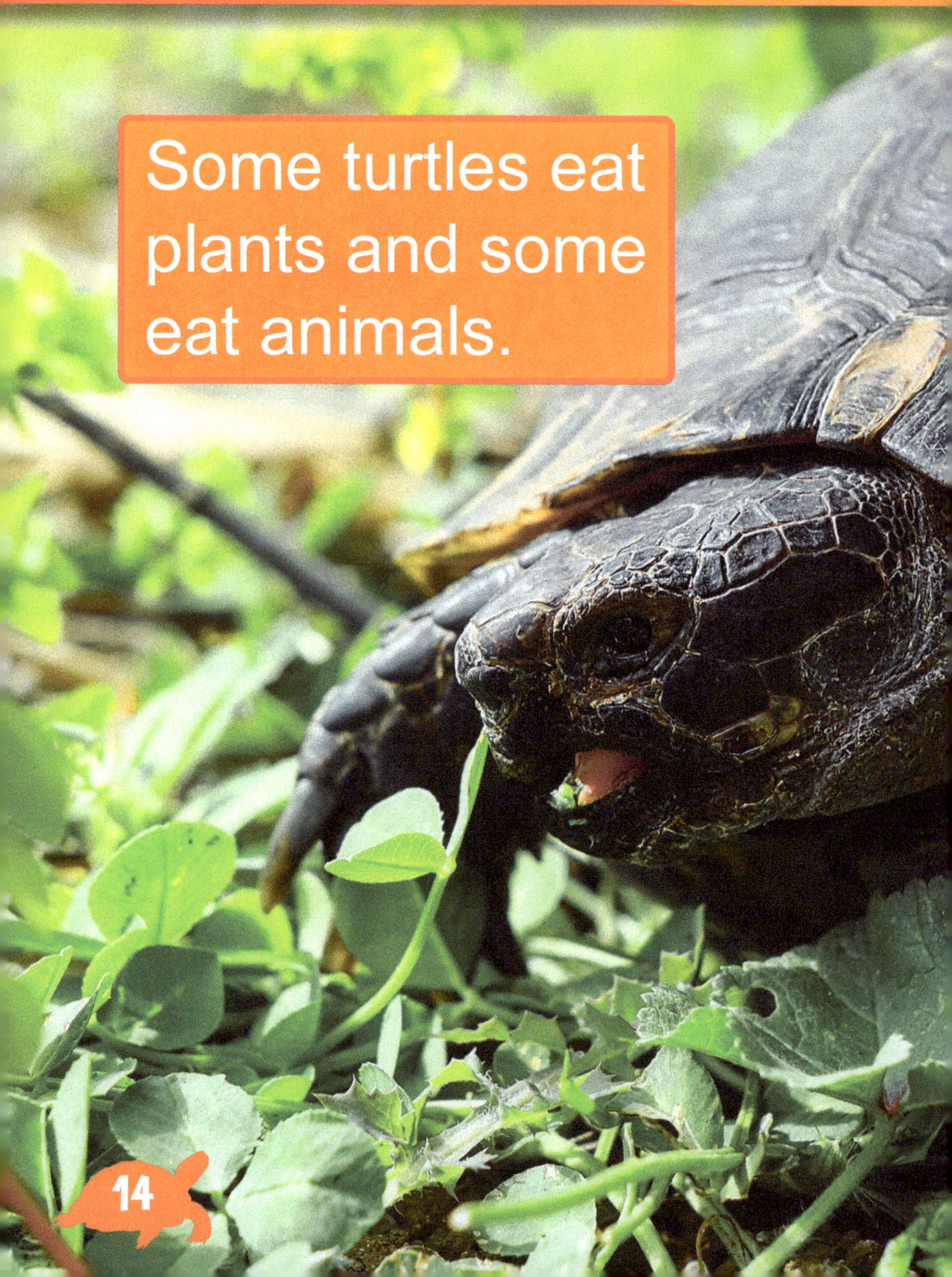

Some turtles eat both plants and animals.

Sea turtles eat seagrass and keep it short.

Seagrass needs to be short to stay healthy.

17

Many animals live in seagrass beds.

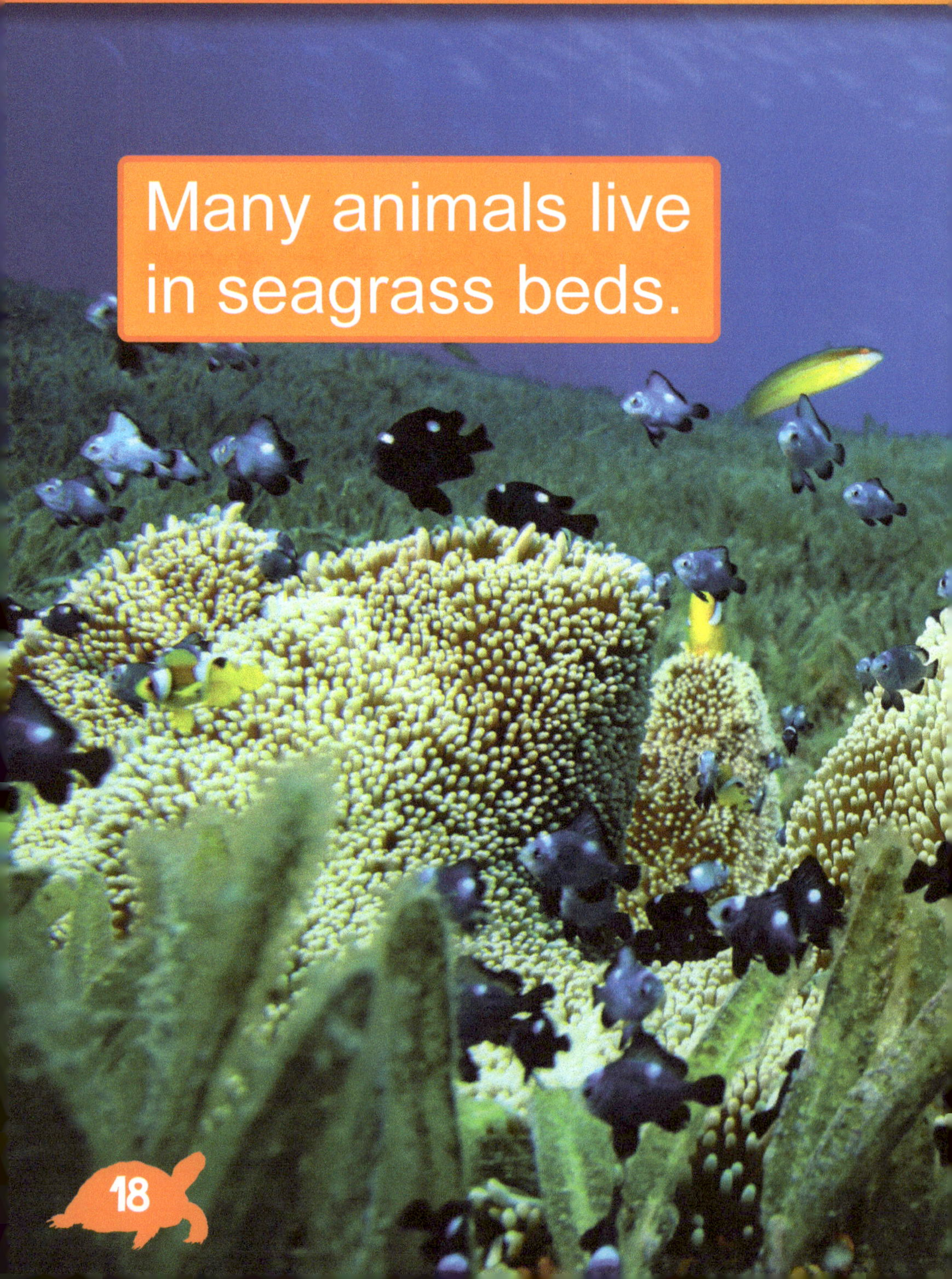

Sea turtles
help keep their
homes healthy.

Turtles lay eggs in the sand.

They lay between one and 200 eggs.

Eggs that do not hatch become food for plants.

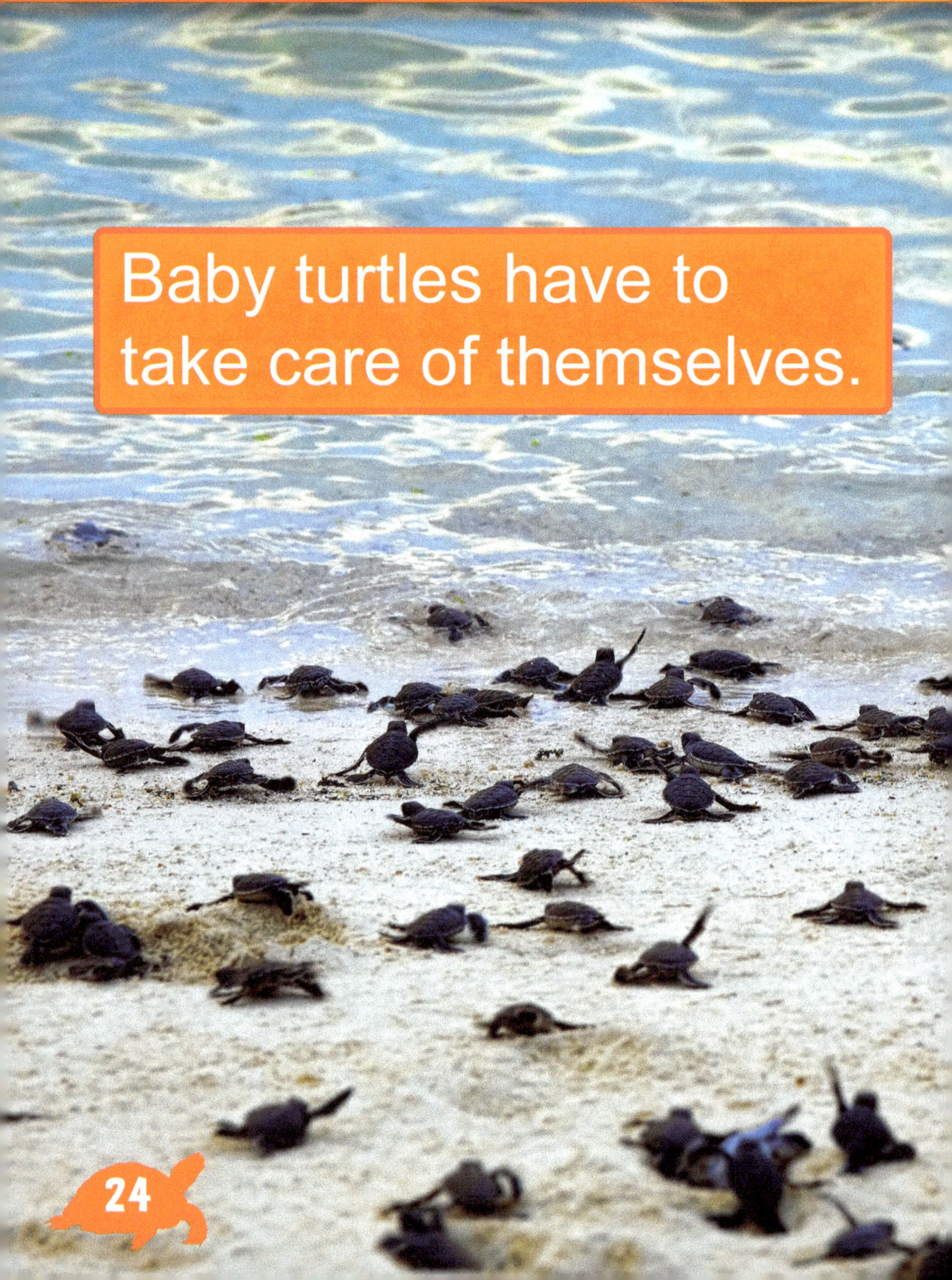

Baby turtles have to take care of themselves.

Some turtles can live for 150 years!

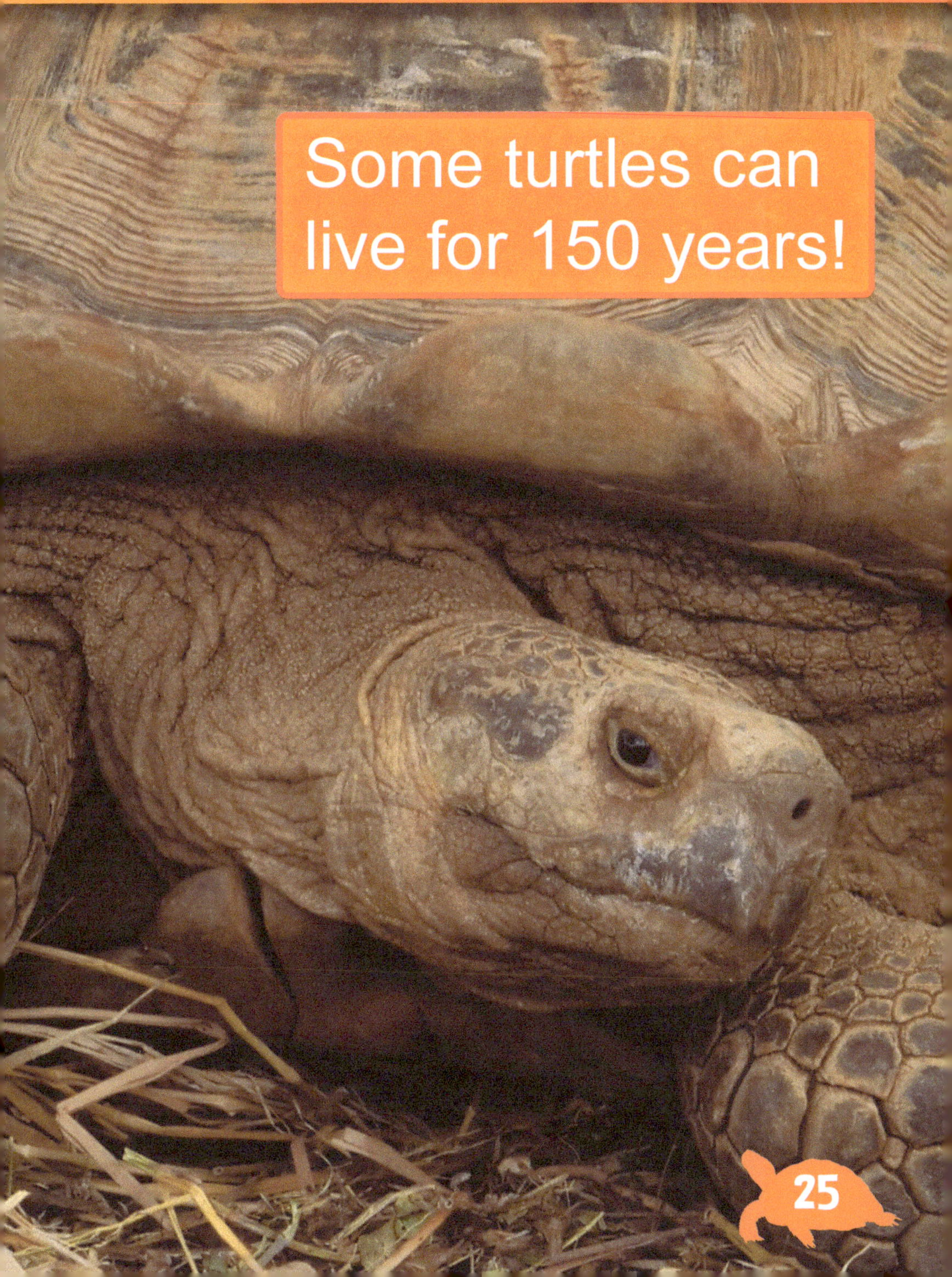

Some turtles are
in danger.

They may not be around
for much longer

27

Many people hunt turtles.

Garbage in the ocean can hurt them.

Quiz

Test your knowledge of turtles by answering the following questions. The questions are based on what you have read in this book. The answers are listed on the bottom of the next page.

1 Can turtle shells be taken off?

2 Do some turtles have thick feet?

3 Does seagrass need to be short to stay healthy?

4 Do turtles lay eggs in the sand?

5 Can some turtles live for 150 years?

6 Are some turtles in danger?

Explore other books in the
Animals That Make a Difference series

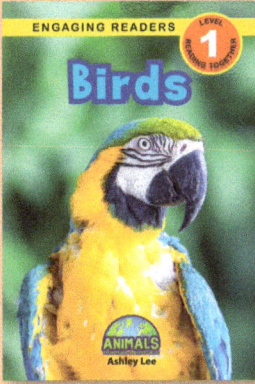

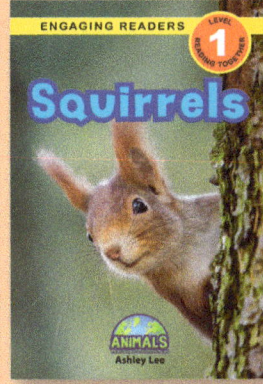

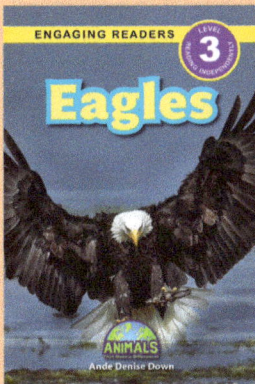
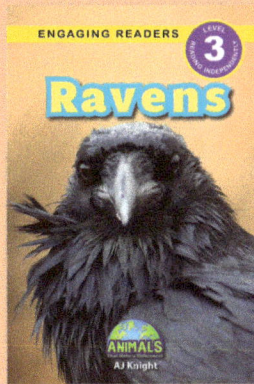
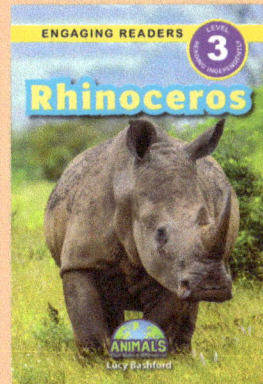

Visit www.engagebooks.com to explore more Engaging Readers.